This Crystal Chronicle belongs to

....

my CRYSTAL CHRONICLE

A record of my gemstone & crystal treasures...

First published by NoooBooks, 2019
Tweed Heads, NSW, Australia.

Printed and bound by your closest POD to reduce waste and Carbon footprint.

If purchased in a bookstore, the paper this book is printed on is certified against
the Forest Stewardship Council ® Standards.
FSC promotes environmentally responsible, socially beneficial and economically
viable management of the world's forests.

ISBN:978-0-6484962-6-7

ONlooolsooks

Contents

⊕INTRODUCTION

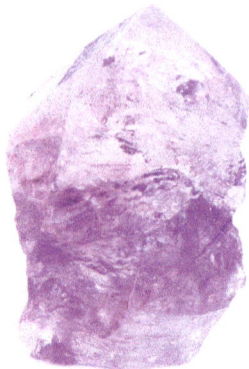

This is your Crystal Chronicle, a book to record your crystal journey and what about each one is noteworthy to you.

Did you find a gem? Was it a gift from a friend? Did you buy it from your favourite Rock shop? Or a new piece of Jewellery? Recording the date, location, price, use, meaning and other special notes may be of benefit to you.

There is no doubt, Crystals ARE amazing. Not only for their striking appearance, but it's fascinating how they were formed, the different combinations and proportions of minerals making them how they are. If you look at their chemistry and molecular structure, their colours and how they make you feel, it is these unique properties that makes them one of Natures' truest gems, Every crystal is beautiful.

At the end is an additional notes section to house your crystal adventures.

I remember the first crystal I bought as a kid like it was yesterday, sadly I have forgotten what some of my crystals are, and that is where this book comes in.

ABOUT THIS BOOK

If you chronicle your crystals over time, this will enhance your connection to your rocks and you will never forget any details about your collection of crystals, gemstones and rock treasures, which grows with you over the rest of your life.

FURTHER RESOURCES

There is alot of information easily available about the use and care of crystals. Take a look through the summary and research what appeals to you. These are a couple of Authors I found particularly good;

* Melody
* Judy Hall
* Doreen Virtue
* Scott Cunningham

SUMMARY OF CRYSTAL USES
- Healing
- Meditation
- Anxiety & Stress release
- Reduce EMR
- Help sleep
- Connection to nature
- Add Nature to your home
- Love of Colour
- Decoration
- Energy vibrations
- Balancing energies
- Protection from negative energies
- Programming/ Manifesting
- Dowsing
- Aura cleansing
- Healing grids
- Rituals
- Do not replace necessary medical treatments

CRYSTAL CARE
Crystals should be kept as dust free as possible and cleansed often by a suitable method to maintain their optimum properties.

Take care as some rocks are damaged by water (e.g Calcite, Selenite, Turquoise, Malachite and many others). Some crystals fade in the sun (e.g amethyst, fossilised corals), and some rocks are toxic.

Some cleaning/re-charging methods include;
- Full Moon light
- Sunlight
- Burying in earth
- Salt water
- Flowing water
- Visualisation
- Other crystals (Carnelian)
- Smudging, candles
- Chemically

Have fun on your unique crystal journey!

MY CRYSTAL CHRONICLE

Date	No#	Name	Page	Date	No#	Name	Page
	1				26		
	2				27		
	3				28		
	4				29		
	5				30		
	6				31		
	7				32		
	8				33		
	9				34		
	10				35		
	11				36		
	12				37		
	13				38		
	14				39		
	15				40		
	16				41		
	17				42		
	18				43		
	19				44		
	20				45		
	21				46		
	22				47		
	23				48		
	24				49		
	25				50		

Date	No#	Name	Page	Date	No#	Name	Page
....	51	....	....	....	76	....	....
....	52	....	....	....	77	....	....
....	53	....	....	....	78	....	....
....	54	....	....	....	79	....	....
....	55	....	....	....	80	....	....
....	56	....	....	....	81	....	....
....	57	....	....	....	82	....	....
....	58	....	....	....	83	....	....
....	59	....	....	....	84	....	....
....	60	....	....	....	85	....	....
....	61	....	....	....	86	....	....
....	62	....	....	....	87	....	....
....	63	....	....	....	88	....	....
....	64	....	....	....	89	....	....
....	65	....	....	....	90	....	....
....	66	....	....	....	91	....	....
....	67	....	....	....	92	....	....
....	68	....	....	....	93	....	....
....	69	....	....	....	94	....	....
....	70	....	....	....	95	....	....
....	71	....	....	....	96	....	....
....	72	....	....	....	97	....	....
....	73	....	....	....	98	....	....
....	74	....	....	....	99	....	....
....	75	....	....	....	100	....	....

❋ MY CRYSTAL CHRONICLE ❋

Date	No#	Name	Page	Date	No#	Name	Page
	101				126		
	102				127		
	103				128		
	104				129		
	105				130		
	106				131		
	107				132		
	108				133		
	109				134		
	110				135		
	111				136		
	112				137		
	113				138		
	114				139		
	115				140		
	116				141		
	117				142		
	118				143		
	119				144		
	120				145		
	121				146		
	122				147		
	123				148		
	124				149		
	125				150		

Date	No#	Name	Page	Date	No#	Name	Page
	151				176		
	152				177		
	153				178		
	154				179		
	155				180		
	156				181		
	157				182		
	158				183		
	159				184		
	160				185		
	161				186		
	162				187		
	163				188		
	164				189		
	165				190		
	166				191		
	167				192		
	168				193		
	169				194		
	170				195		
	171				196		
	172				197		
	173				198		
	174				199		
	175				200		

☀ MY 𝕮RYSTAL 𝕮HRONICLE ☀

Date	No#	Name	Page	Date	No#	Name	Page
	201				226		
	202				227		
	203				228		
	204				229		
	205				230		
	206				231		
	207				232		
	208				233		
	209				234		
	210				235		
	211				236		
	212				237		
	213				238		
	214				239		
	215				240		
	216				241		
	217				242		
	218				243		
	219				244		
	220				245		
	221				246		
	222				247		
	223				248		
	224				249		
	225				250		

Date	No#	Name	Page	Date	No#	Name	Page
	251				276		
	252				277		
	253				278		
	254				279		
	255				280		
	256				281		
	257				282		
	258				283		
	259				284		
	260				285		
	261				286		
	262				287		
	263				288		
	264				289		
	265				290		
	266				291		
	267				292		
	268				293		
	269				294		
	270				295		
	271				296		
	272				297		
	273				298		
	274				299		
	275				300		

MY CRYSTAL CHRONICLE

Date	No#	Name	Page	Date	No#	Name	Page
	301				326		
	302				327		
	303				3 28		
	304				329		
	305				330		
	306				331		
	307				332		
	308				333		
	309				334		
	310				335		
	311				336		
	312				337		
	313				338		
	314				339		
	315				340		
	316				341		
	317				342		
	318				343		
	319				344		
	320				345		
	321				346		
	322				347		
	323				348		
	324				349		
	325				350		

Date	No#	Name	Page	Date	No#	Name	Page
	351				376		
	352				377		
	353				378		
	354				379		
	355				380		
	356				381		
	357				382		
	358				383		
	359				384		
	360				385		
	361				386		
	362				387		
	363				388		
	364				389		
	365				390		
	366				391		
	367				392		
	368				393		
	369				394		
	370				395		
	371				396		
	372				397		
	373				398		
	374				399		
	375				400		

CLEAR STONES

⚙ CLEAR STONES

Red Stones

⊛ RED STONES

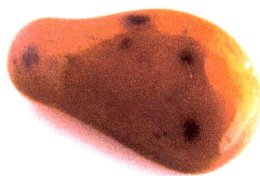

☉ RED STONES

⊛ RED STONES

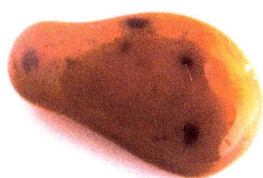

ORANGE STONES

⚙ ORANGE STONES

⚜ ORANGE STONES

44

Yellow Stones

◉ YELLOW STONES

YELLOW STONES

YELLOW STONES

YELLOW STONES

Green Stones

⊛ GREEN STONES

BLUE
STONES

BLUE STONES

Violet, Pink & Purple Stones

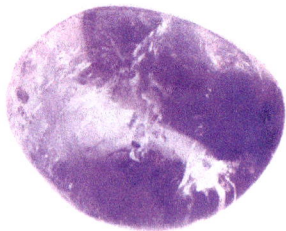

VIOLET, PURPLE & PINK STONES

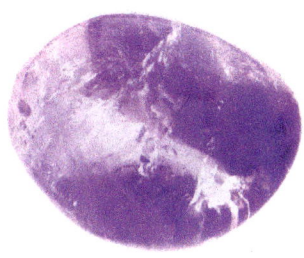

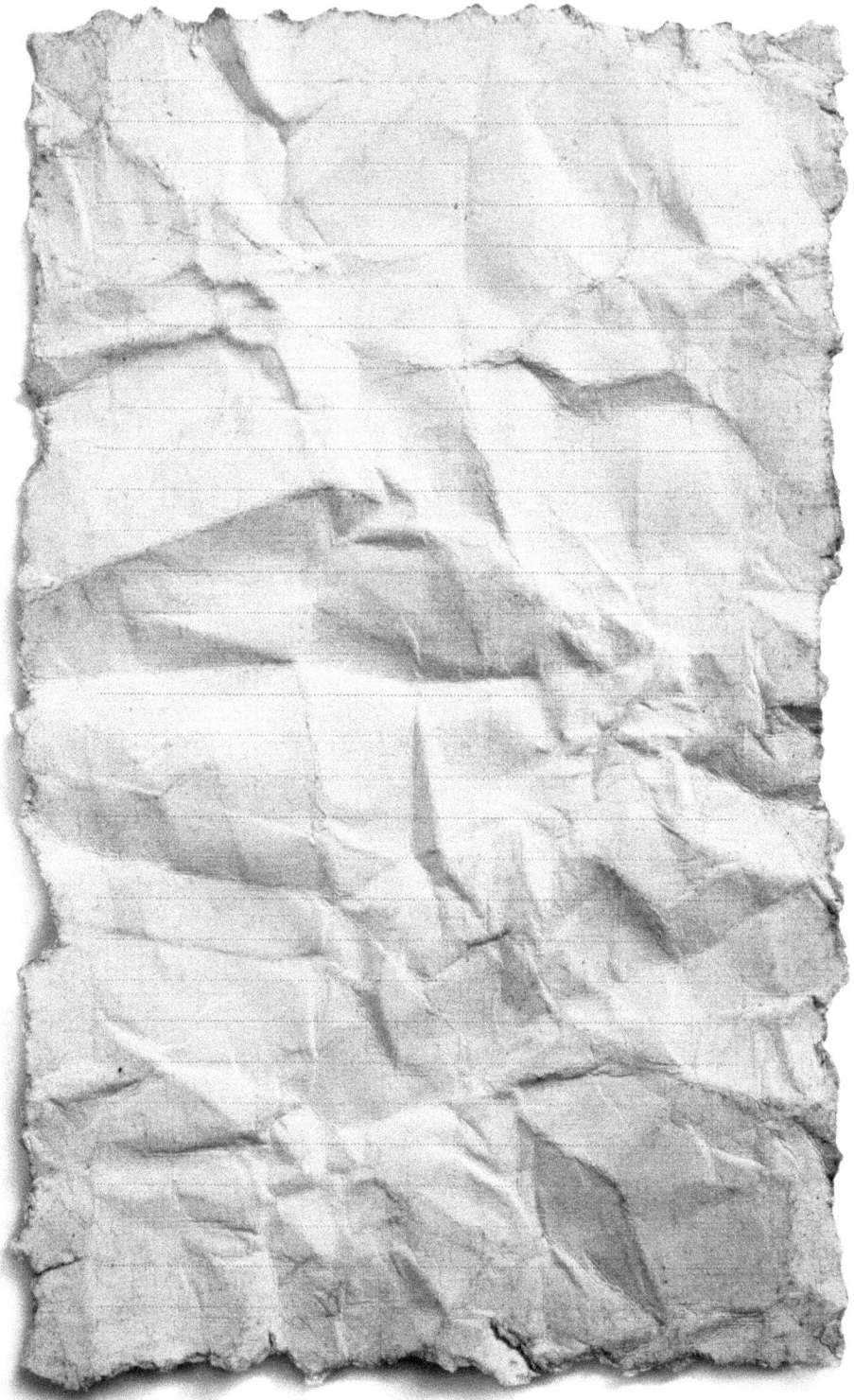

BLACK, WHITE & GREY STONES

⊛ BLACK, WHITE & GREY STONES

⊛ BLACK, WHITE & GREY STONES

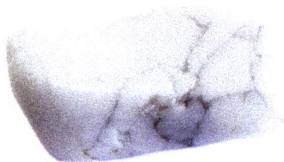

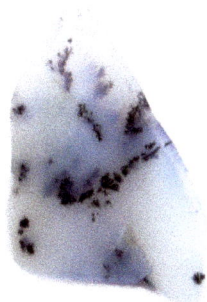

⊛ BLACK, WHITE & GREY STONES

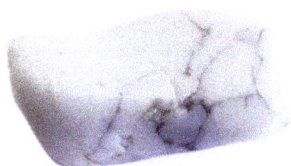

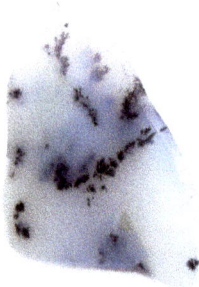

EARTH TONE STONES

....
....
....
....
....
....
....
....
....

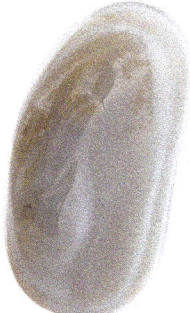

⊛EARTH TONE STONES

⊕EARTH TONE STONES

MULTI-COLOURED STONES

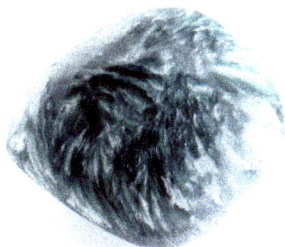

My Stones

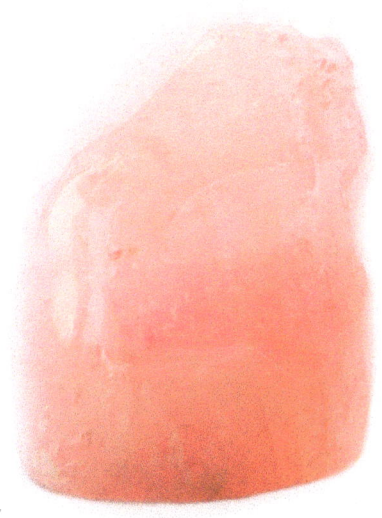

❀STONES

STONES

✸ STONES

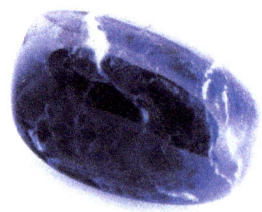

❀ PHOTO LIST

*Crystals named here are
believed to be correct,
if there are errors
please let us know.

If only the owner of these
crystals had this book earlier!

INDEX

A

B

C

D

E

F

G

H

I

J

K

L

M

N

O

P

INDEX

Q

R

S

T

U

V

W

X

www.ingramcontent.com/pod-product-compliance
Lightning Source LLC
Chambersburg PA
CBHW051618030426
42334CB00030B/3247